Published by Mz. Kim Productions
4263 Tierra Rejada Rd #151
Moorpark, CA 93021
www.mzkimproductions.com

ISBN: 978-1-962106-06-1

Printed in United States of America
First Printing: August 2023
Date of Copyright: July 5,2023
Cover design by Marina Trapanese
Illustrations by Marina Trapanese
Edited by Joshua Nickel

For permissions, please contact: Mz. Kim Productions
4263 Tierra Rejada Rd #151
Moorpark, CA 93021
www.mzkimproductions.com
mzkimproductions@gmail.com

Dedication Page:

To all the children who seek hope and love,
This book is dedicated to you.
May it bring joy to your hearts,
Inspire curiosity and empathy too.

To Grandma Margie,
Whose stories are filled with wisdom and grace.
Thank you for sharing your tales with us,
And teaching us about love's embrace.

To Zipporah and Zion,
Whose eager hearts and curious minds,
Bring life to every page and line,
May your thirst for knowledge never decline.

To the Samaritan woman at the well,
Whose story echoes through the ages.
May her journey inspire us all,
To find hope in life's many stages.

And to Jesus, our everlasting guide,
Whose love quenches our deepest thirst.
May his message of hope and grace,
Forever in our hearts be immersed.

With love and gratitude,
Dr. K.T. Zulkowski

Author Note:

Dear Readers,

It is with great excitement and gratitude that I present to you this book. As the author, I have poured my heart and soul into crafting a story that will captivate and inspire readers of all ages.

This book is a culmination of my lifelong passion for storytelling and my dedication to spreading positive messages through literature. I have always believed in the power of books to transport us to different worlds, to teach us valuable lessons, and to ignite our imaginations. It is my hope that this book accomplishes all of those things and more.

I am deeply indebted to the countless individuals who have supported me on this journey. To my family and friends, thank you for your unwavering encouragement and belief in my abilities. To my editor and publisher, thank you for your guidance and for helping me shape this story into its best version.

I would also like to express my gratitude to the readers who have embraced my previous works. Your kind words and feedback have fueled my passion for writing and have pushed me to continue sharing stories that touch hearts and minds.

Lastly, I want to dedicate this book to the children who are the primary audience for this story. It is my hope that through this tale, they will find solace, inspiration, and hope. May they see themselves reflected in the characters, and may they be encouraged to embrace their uniqueness and pursue their dreams with unwavering determination.

Thank you for joining me on this literary adventure. I am honored to have you as a reader, and I hope that this book brings you joy, laughter, and a renewed sense of wonder.

With warmest regards,

Dr. KT. Zulkowski

Educational Value:

This book holds significant educational value as it introduces young readers to a significant biblical story and its relevance in their lives. By immersing children in the vibrant illustrations and relatable dialogue, the book helps them understand Jesus' compassion and the impact of his love. It also teaches empathy, curiosity, and the importance of sharing stories and experiences with others.

In the story, Grandma Margie gathers Zipporah and Zion around her cozy armchair, creating a warm and inviting atmosphere. They are surrounded by books and toys, symbolizing the joy of storytelling and learning. As Grandma Margie begins the tale, the children's faces fill with excitement and anticipation.

The journey begins as Grandma Margie, Zipporah, and Zion walk hand in hand through a vibrant landscape of rolling hills and a winding path. This visual representation of the journey mirrors the adventure and discovery that awaits them in the story. Zipporah curiously asks where they are going, and Grandma Margie explains that they are embarking on a journey to Samaria, just like Jesus did in the Bible.

Upon reaching their destination, the bustling marketplace with a central well comes to life through the illustrations. Zipporah and Zion's eyes widen as they watch Grandma Margie point to the well, where a weary woman with a water jar stands. The woman's face reveals weariness and longing, prompting Zion to ask about her. Grandma Margie explains that the woman is searching for something more than just water. She introduces John 4:10, where Jesus tells the woman that if she knew the gift of God and who was asking for a drink, she would have asked him, and he would have given her living water.

As the story unfolds, the woman sits by the well, accompanied by Grandma Margie, Zipporah, and Zion. Their faces reflect curiosity and empathy as they observe the scene. Grandma Margie explains that the woman's sadness stems from a thirst in her heart that only Jesus can quench. She quotes John 4:14, where Jesus promises that whoever drinks the water he gives will never thirst again but will have a spring of water welling up to eternal life.

The pivotal moment arrives as the illustrations depict Jesus, dressed in a white robe, sitting beside the woman at the well. His compassionate eyes meet hers as he offers her the gift of living water. Grandma Margie, Zipporah, and Zion watch in awe and wonder. Zion, filled with curiosity, asks Grandma Margie about the gift Jesus is giving. Grandma Margie explains that Jesus is offering the water of eternal life, a love that will never run dry. She quotes John 4:13-14, where Jesus explains that while everyone who drinks ordinary water will be thirsty again, those who drink the water he gives will never thirst, and it will become a spring of water welling up to eternal life within them.

The story concludes with the woman, now filled with joy and excitement, leaving her water jar behind and running back to her village. Grandma Margie, Zipporah, and Zion follow her, their faces beaming with happiness and anticipation. Zipporah remarks on the woman's newfound happiness, and Grandma Margie explains that Jesus has transformed her heart and filled her with joy. The woman shares her story with her fellow villagers, and Grandma Margie and the children listen attentively. The final illustration shows Grandma Margie, Zipporah, and Zion standing in the village square, surrounded by a crowd of people. They are captivated by the woman's testimony and the power of Jesus' love, fostering unity and joy among them.

Through the captivating narrative and vibrant illustrations, "Grandma Margie's Tale of The Well of Hope" not only introduces young readers to a significant biblical story but also teaches essential values such as empathy, curiosity, and the importance of sharing stories and experiences. It creates a warm and inviting atmosphere that encourages children to engage with the story, fostering a love for reading and learning. Additionally, the book promotes understanding of Jesus' message of love and his transformative power, inspiring children to seek hope and fulfillment in their own lives.

Grandma Margie's Tale of the Well of Hope

Grandma Margie: "Gather around, my dear Zippo-rah and Zion. It's storytime!
Today, I want to share with you a beautiful story from the Bible."

Zipporah: *"Where are we going, Grandma?"*

Grandma Margie: *"We're going on a journey to Samaria, just like Jesus did in the Bible.*

Let me share with you a scripture from John 4:4: 'And he had to pass through Samaria.'"

Zion: *"Who is that, Grandma?"*

Grandma Margie: *"That, my dear Zion, is a woman who is searching for something more than just water.*

In John 4:10, Jesus said to her,
'If you knew the gift of God and who it is that asks you for a drink, you would have asked him and he would have given you living water.'"

Zipporah: *"Why does she look so sad, Grandma?"*

Grandma Margie: *"She has a thirst in her heart that only Jesus can quench, my sweet Zipporah.*

In John 4:14, Jesus said,
'But whoever drinks the water I give them will never thirst. Indeed, the water I give them will become in them a spring of water welling up to eternal life.'"

Zion: *"What is Jesus giving her, Grandma?"*

Grandma Margie: *"He is offering her the water of eternal life, a love that will never run dry.*

In John 4:13-14, Jesus said,
'Everyone who drinks this water will be thirsty again, but whoever drinks the water I give them will never thirst. Indeed, the water I give them will become in them a spring of water welling up to eternal life.'"

Zipporah: *"Look, Grandma! The woman is so happy now!"*

Grandma Margie: *"Yes, my dear Zipporah. Jesus has transformed her heart and filled her with joy.*

In John 4:29, the woman said to her fellow villagers, 'Come, see a man who told me everything I ever did. Could this be the Messiah?'"

Zion: *"Why are they all listening, Grandma?"*

Grandma Margie: *"They are listening to the woman's story of how Jesus changed her life. They want to know about the living water too.*

In John 4:39, it says,
'Many of the Samaritans from that town believed in him because of the woman's testimony.'"

The End

It's wasn't The water. He car

for,it was me.

-woman at the well

www.ingramcontent.com/pod-product-compliance
Lightning Source LLC
Chambersburg PA
CBHW041531120626
46551CB00018B/2659